If you were me and lived in...
RENAISSANCE ITALY

Carole P. Roman
Illustrated by Silvia Brunetti
With accompanying illustrations by Kelsea Wierenga

For Hallie- you amaze me.

Special thanks to my wonderful assistant, Brittney Bass.

Book Design by Kelsea Wierenga

Copyright © 2016 Carole P. Roman

All rights reserved.

ISBN-13: 978-1523234271

If you were me and lived in...
RENAISSANCE ITALY

If you were me and lived in Renaissance (Ren-ai-san-ce) Italy, you would have been born over five hundred years ago around the year 1483, somewhere outside of Florence, Italy, in a region called Tuscany (Tus-ca-nee). Italy is in the southern portion of Europe.

Firenze

This is Florence today and the following page is a painting of Florence from the 1400s.

What are the major differences? Has the city changed in any way?

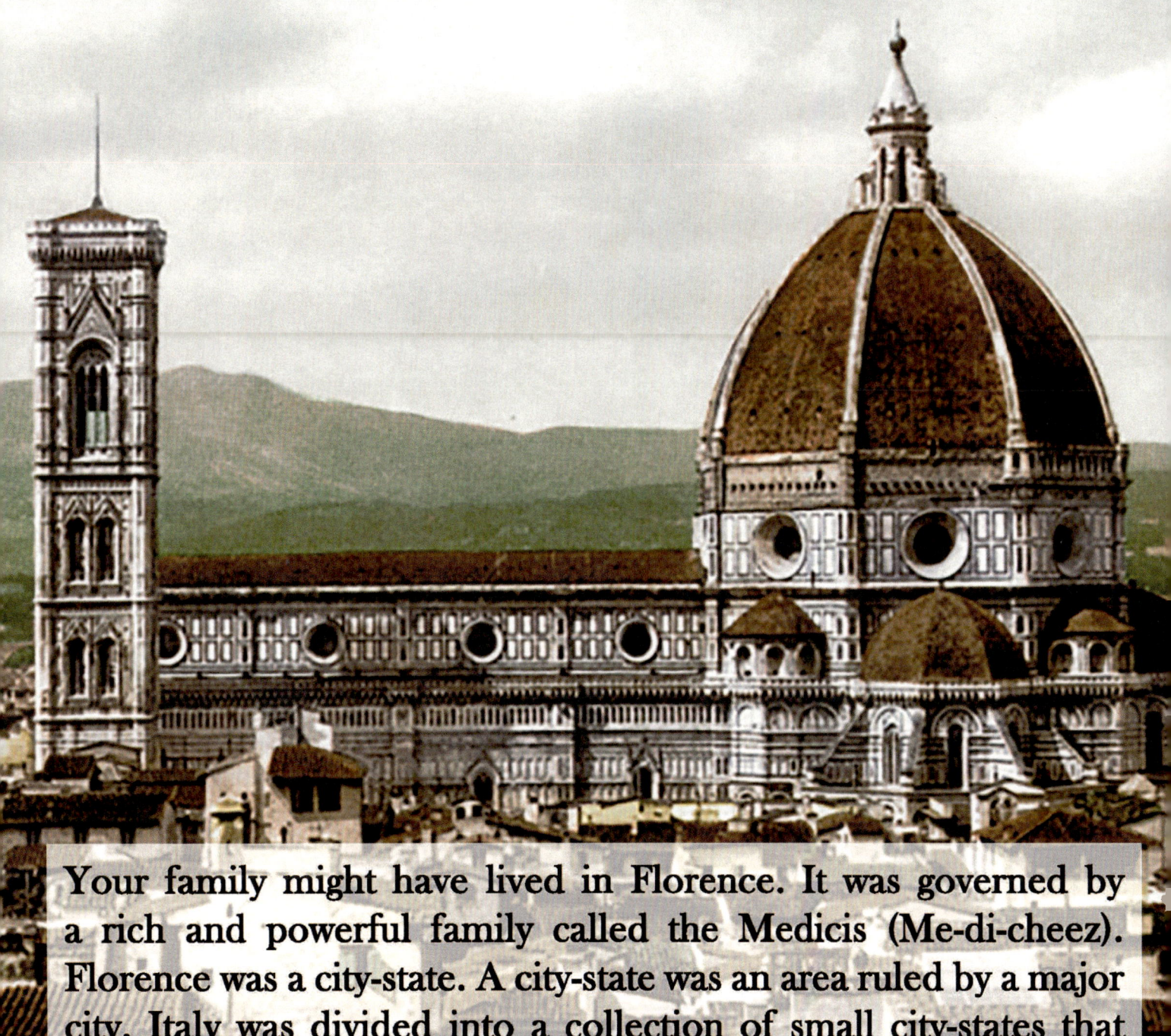

Your family might have lived in Florence. It was governed by a rich and powerful family called the Medicis (Me-di-cheez). Florence was a city-state. A city-state was an area ruled by a major city. Italy was divided into a collection of small city-states that were governed by either an elected leader or a ruling family. You would have called your town "Firenze" (Fi-ren-ze).

Your name could have been Dolce (Dohl-chey) or Lisabetta (Liz-a-bet-ta) if you were a girl. Your parents could have chosen Lorenzo (Luh-renz-oh) and Cosimo (Coh-zi-mo) for your brothers' names.

7

The whole world was emerging from the Medieval (Med-eve-val) or Middle Ages. People were poor and farmed land that belonged to the local ruler. They owned very little and didn't have much to spare. They never journeyed far from their home because travel was hard and roads were unsafe. Many highways were unprotected and robbers roamed freely. It was a dangerous time.

Most children did not go to school. Towns were isolated and ideas were rarely exchanged. Diseases were widespread, and sometimes an outbreak could destroy an entire town. Life was slow to change and seemed stagnant for hundreds of years.

A new age was coming. You wouldn't know this time period would be called by a special name, and it was about to change the entire world. It was going to be called the Renaissance and means rebirth in French. People looked back and rediscovered the teachings of Ancient Greece and Rome.

They copied the style of Classical Greece, changing the way people appeared in the artwork. They made everything look more realistic.

The Renaissance was the reawakening of human creativity after a darker time period.

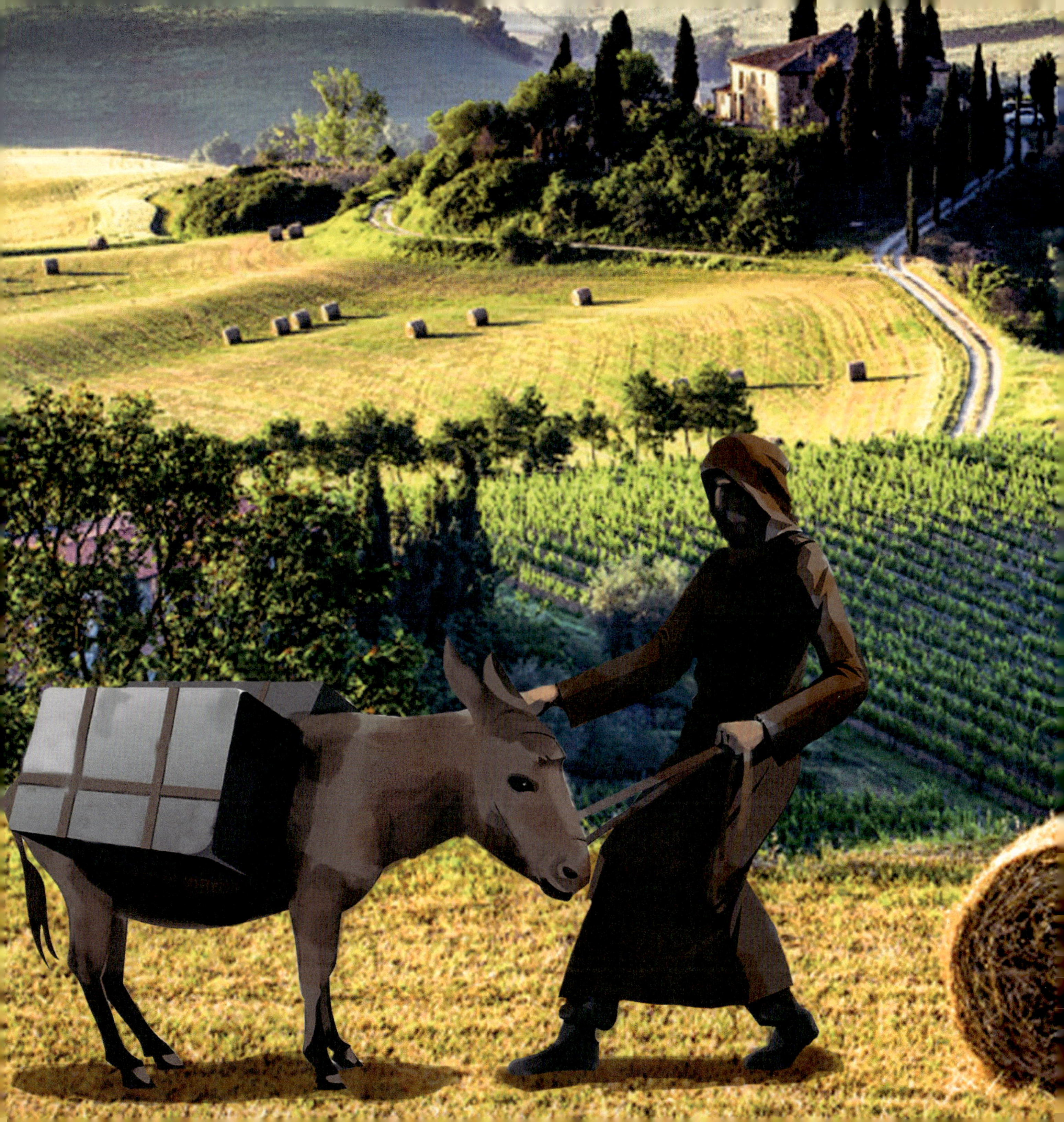

It was an exciting time. Life was changing from art to literature. Architecture took on daring new styles. Science and astronomy were looked at from a new point of view. Exploration of places in the world brought back undiscovered spices, plants, and animals. People became rich from all the new products coming back.

A new class of people called merchants emerged. They made a lot of money and wanted to spend it on making their homes beautiful. They hired artists to paint pictures in the newest styles. Many of these artists were born near your home. Tuscany became the birthplace of this new movement. Your city, Florence, was known as "The Athens of the Middle Ages."

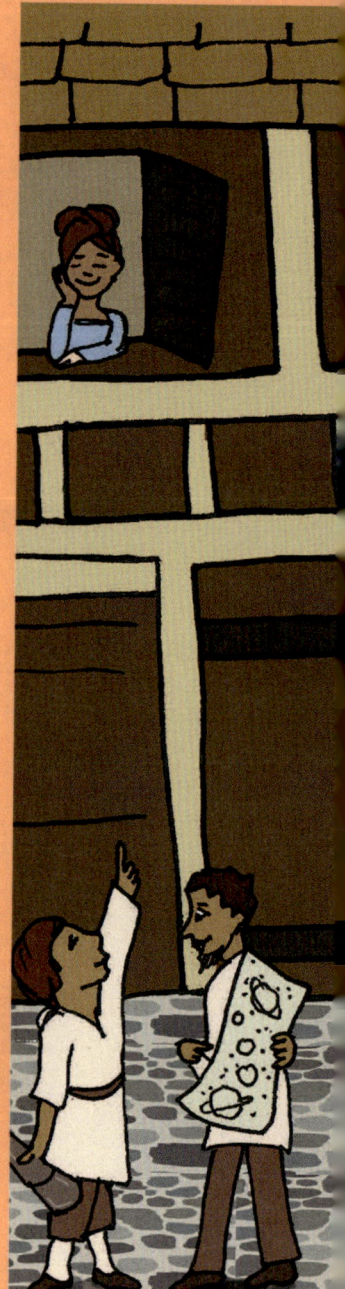

11

Florence was a busy city. It was an important trading and banking center. The Medici (Me-di-chee) family owned the largest bank in Europe and were wealthy. They used their money to pay artists to create beautiful paintings and sculptures. They encouraged them to create new buildings that were different from the old gothic styles. The designs changed from the complicated and ornate concepts to the classical style of ancient Greece and Rome. The Medicis supported famous artists such as Da Vinci (Da Vin-chee), Michelangelo (Mike-ale-an-gel-o), Raphael (Ra-fay-ale), and Donatello (Don-a-tel-lo).

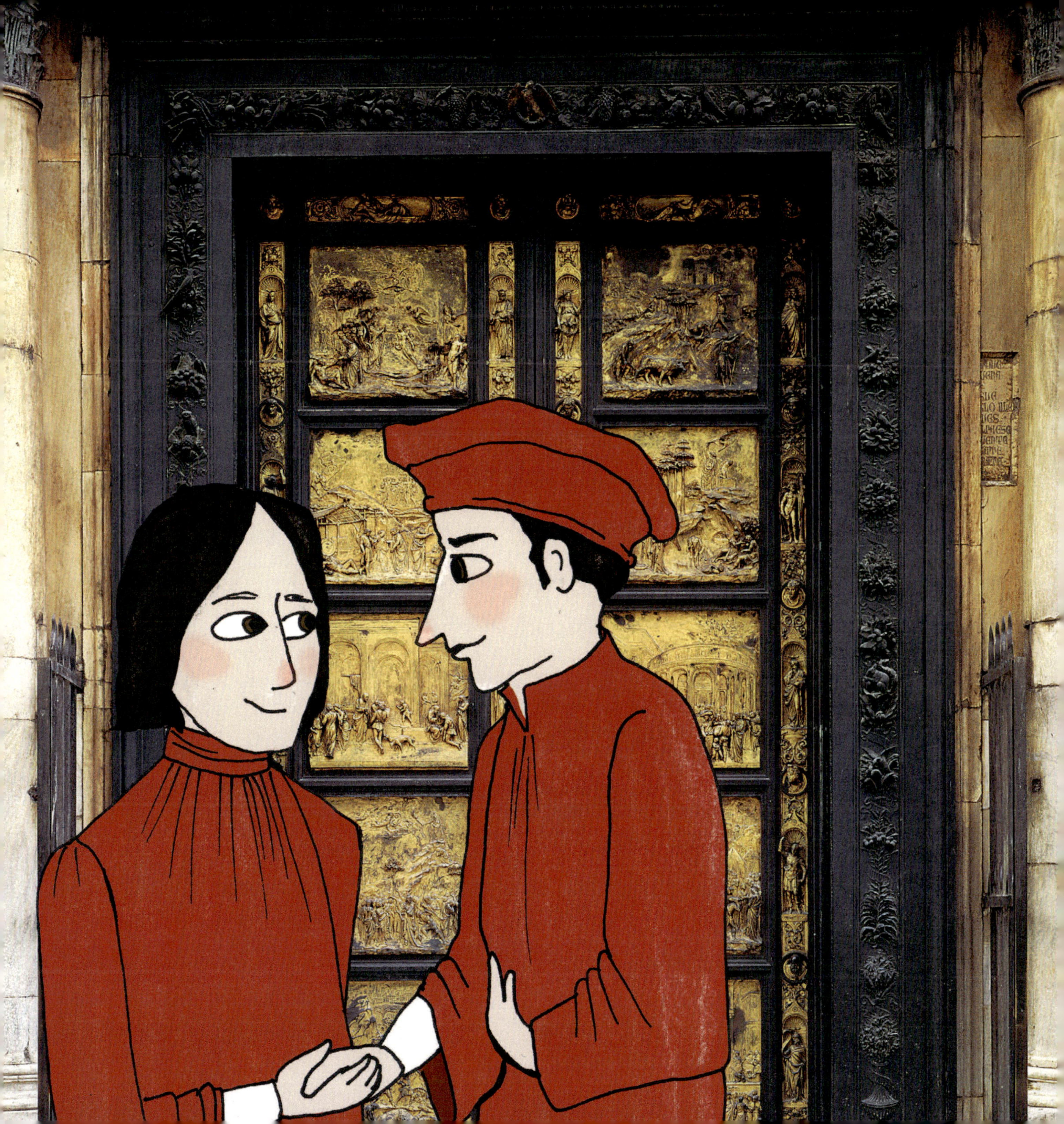

You might have lived in a home called a palazzo (pa-lah-tzo). It had many different levels with high ceilings for air to circulate and keep the home cool in the summertime.

On the ground floor, there would be a heavy wooden double door surrounded by dramatic arches. It would open to a large space called a loggia (law-jah) where your father worked as a merchant. He kept a storeroom in the back filled with all the silks and other materials sold by his business. The ceilings were tall and vaulted, which meant they were rounded with peaks and arches.

You loved to climb up the stone stairway to the second floor where you lived with your family. You shared a room with your three sisters while your five brothers were across the hall. The banister and railings were made from wood and could be taken off if you wanted to keep anyone from coming upstairs uninvited.

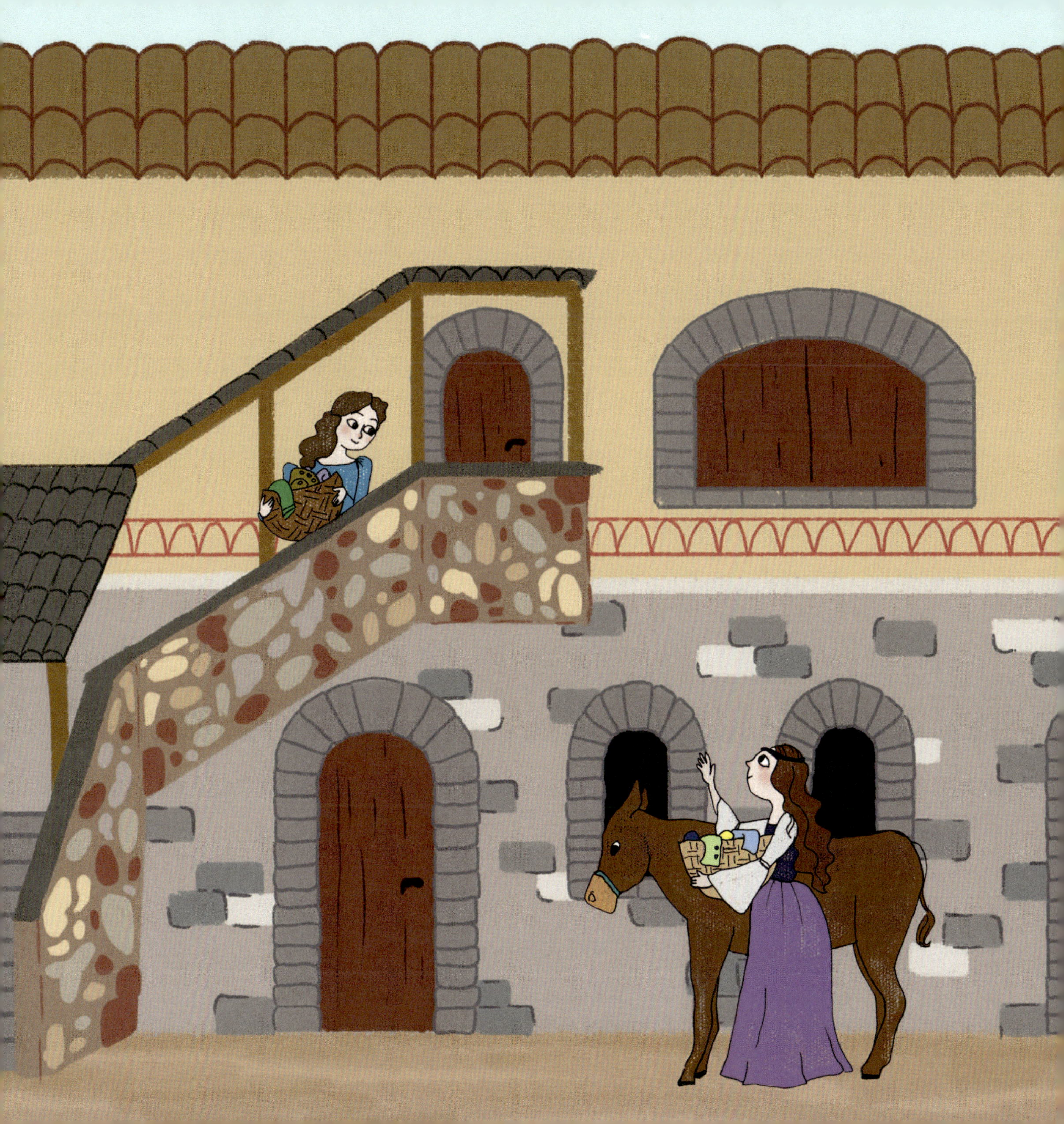

The front room belonged to your papa for business. There was a hole in the second-story floor so he could watch who entered his shop. You were not allowed into this room. It was where he kept all his bills and important letters. Behind a secret door, there was a giant strongbox that held all his money.

Next came the sala (sah-la) or salon, with its big fireplace and high wooden ceiling. This was where the family gathered for meals. There was a large wooden table. You loved the fresco (fres-ko) painting on the wall. Mama hired an artist who spread plaster and painted colorful scenes from the Bible on its rough surface. You never got tired of looking at the faces in the painting.

Beyond that was the bathroom with its hole in the floor for – well – you know what. On the second floor were all the bedrooms including one with a towering, wide bed that you shared with your sisters.

Up another flight of stairs were the kitchen and rooms for the servants. It was the hottest part of the house, and you were glad you didn't have to go up there.

There were lots of arched windows so you could call down to your friends on the streets.

Kitchen   Room for servant

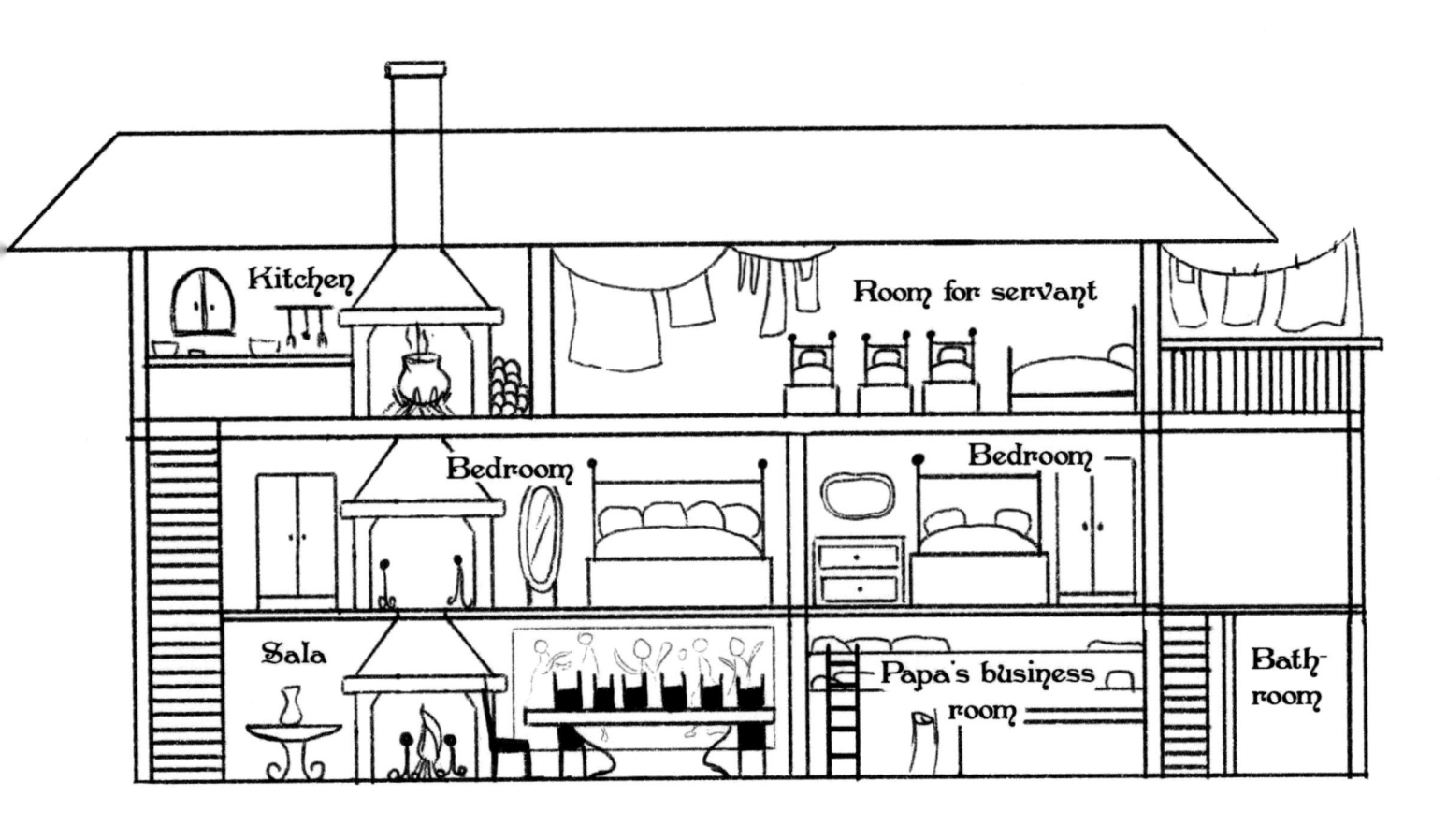

Bedroom   Bedroom

Sala   Papa's business room   Bathroom

17

Your brothers started their education with a tutor who taught them grammar and arithmetic. Soon they were sent to private school where they studied philosophy, Latin, and public speaking, so they would learn to be good citizens.

Mama hired a tutor for you too, but your studies were about being an efficient housewife. Still, there were classes on art, music, and dancing which made the lessons in needlepoint easier to learn. You had to sit for hours, making decorative embroidered pictures that would be put on the walls and chair seats or used as altar cloths. At least you were able to study some classes, unlike the servant girls who never had any opportunity to learn things other than housework.

Your cook seasoned the food with cinnamon, cloves, nutmeg, saffron, and pepper, making your mouth water thinking about the delicious macaroni and rabbit stew. She used oranges and lemons from your orchard in the country to flavor the sauces, and her stuffed pasta was the best in town. She made noodles every day, then filled them with cheeses she bought in the marketplace, baking them in the hot ovens.

You drank ale or watered wine with your meal because everybody knew water was very dangerous to drink. You could get all kinds of illnesses from it.

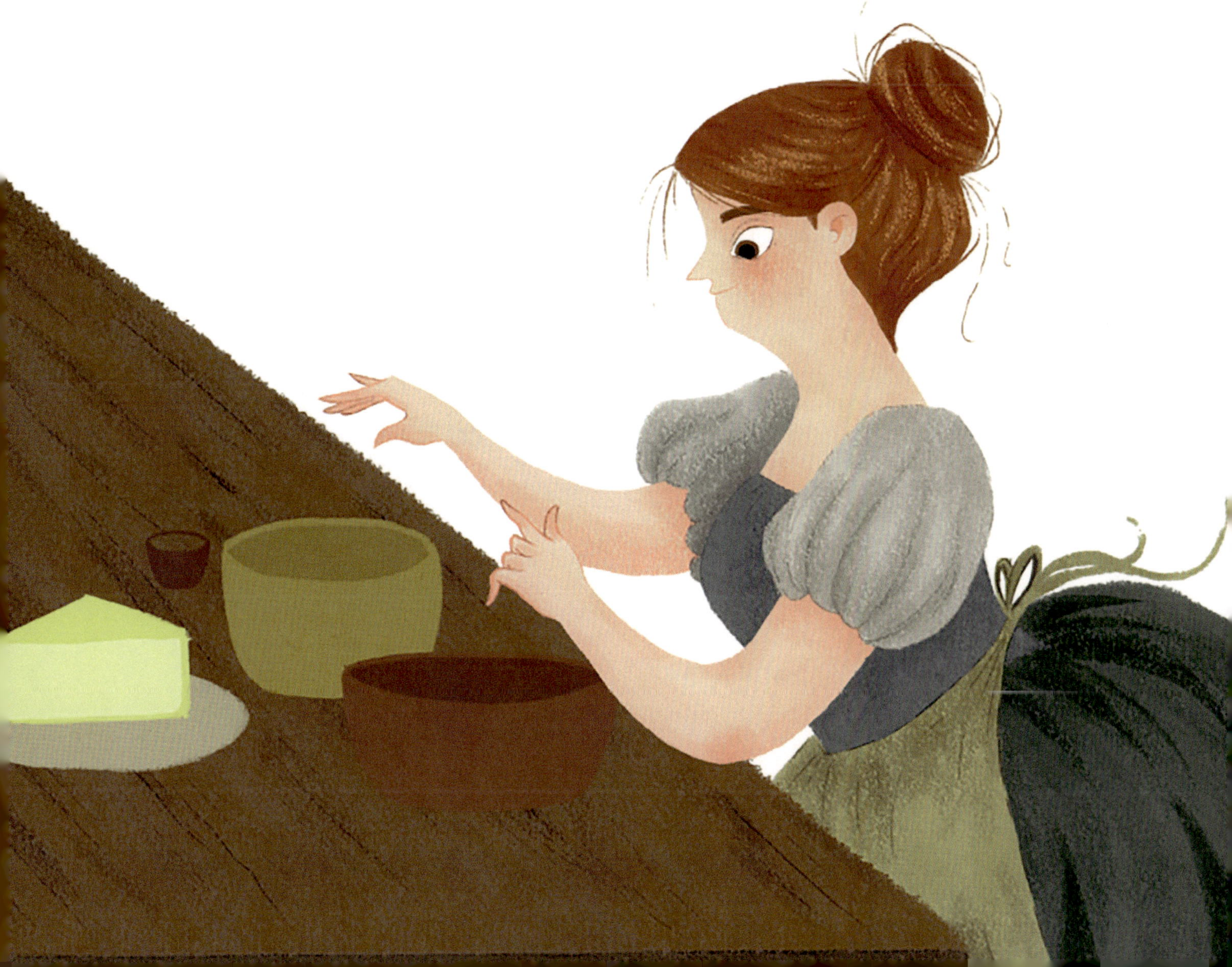

Instead of the dark bread, beans, and pasta which poor workers or farmers had to eat, your family table groaned with lots of meats and new foods like potatoes and peppers that came all the way from across the sea.

On feast days, your cook roasted swans and peacocks and put the feathers back on so when she served them, they looked like they were still alive.

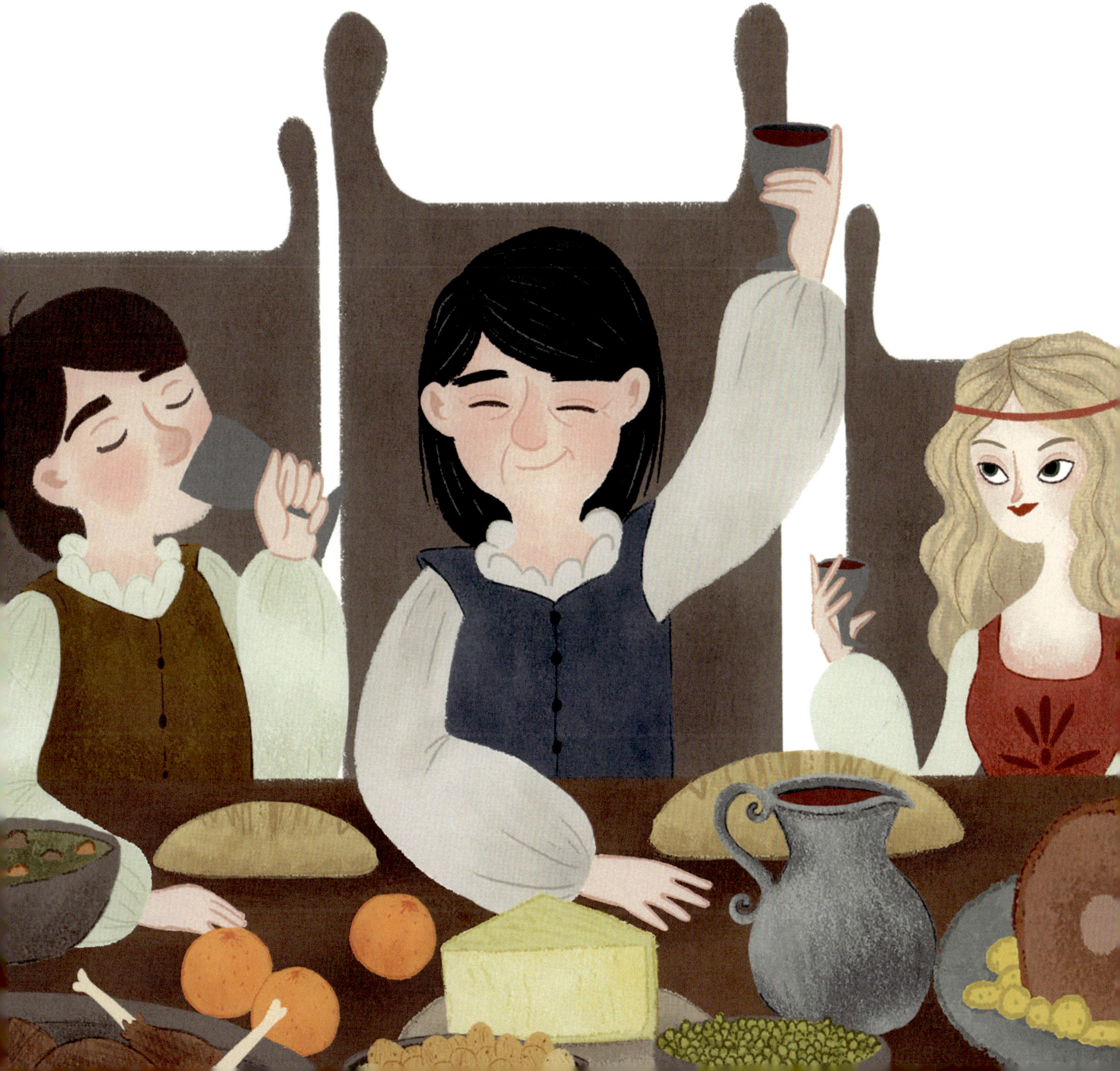

You always ate your meals with another person, sharing the precious two-prong fork and using real wooden plates, instead of hard bread as a trencher or platter like the servants did. Grandfather had a plate made from porcelain or china, and you loved to look at the delicate patterns painted on its beautiful surface. You were not allowed to touch it. It came from the Far East and was fragile; it could easily crack.

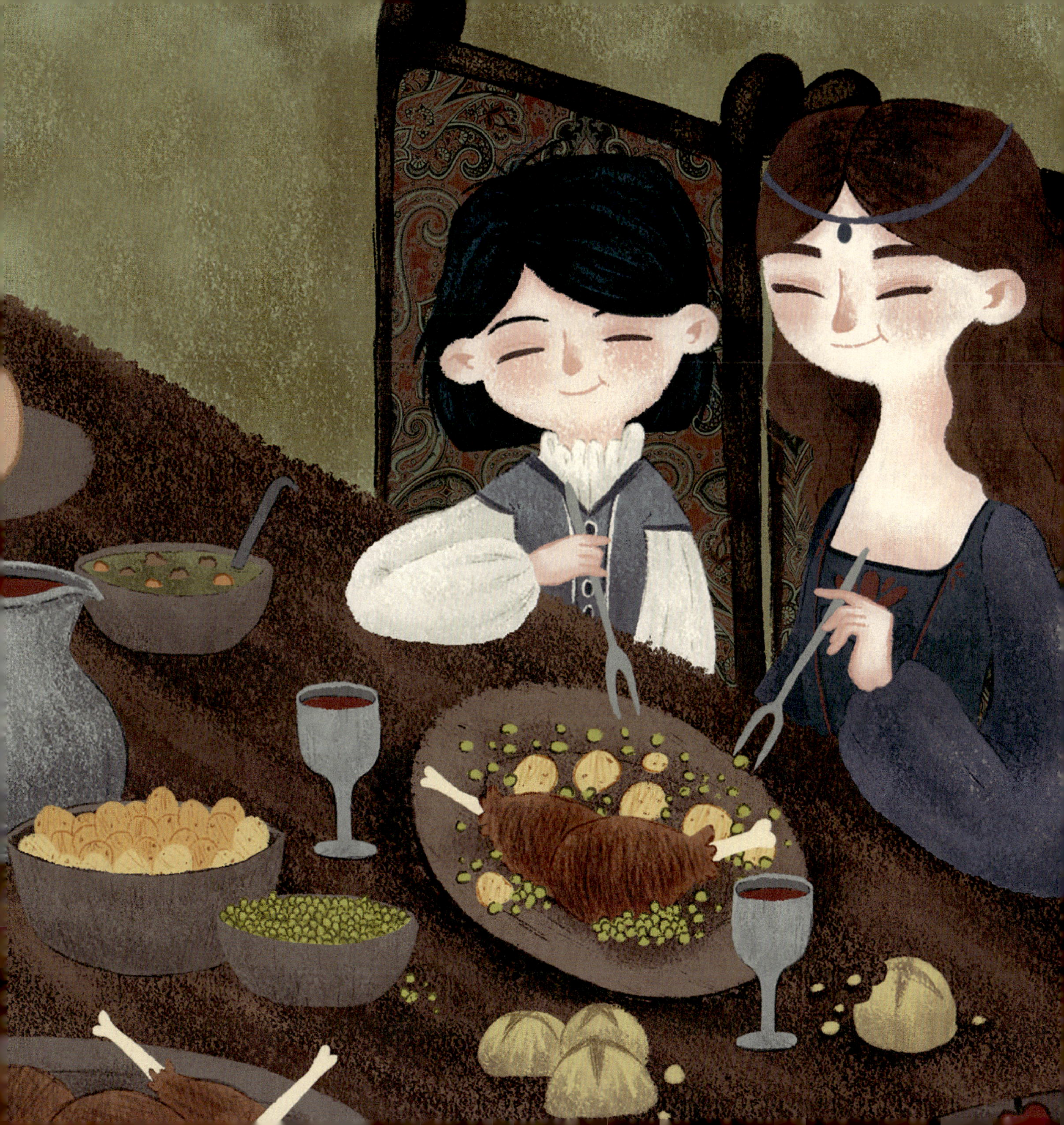

You loved to go shopping in the marketplace in town, but you were not allowed to go anywhere but to church or visit family. You couldn't go out without a nursemaid. You thought you were too old for her, but Papa insisted she had to be with you. When you turned twelve, you knew your parents would be looking for a match for you. You would soon be betrothed (bi-trawtht) to someone special and married by the time you turned sixteen. Your future husband would be much older than you, and your parents planned to give him a dowry (dow-uh-ree) when you married. A dowry was a sum of money that the groom used to invest in his estate or business.

Even though your parents watched over you like a hawk, they didn't treat you like a baby or coddle you. You were dressed like an adult at an early age and expected to act like one.

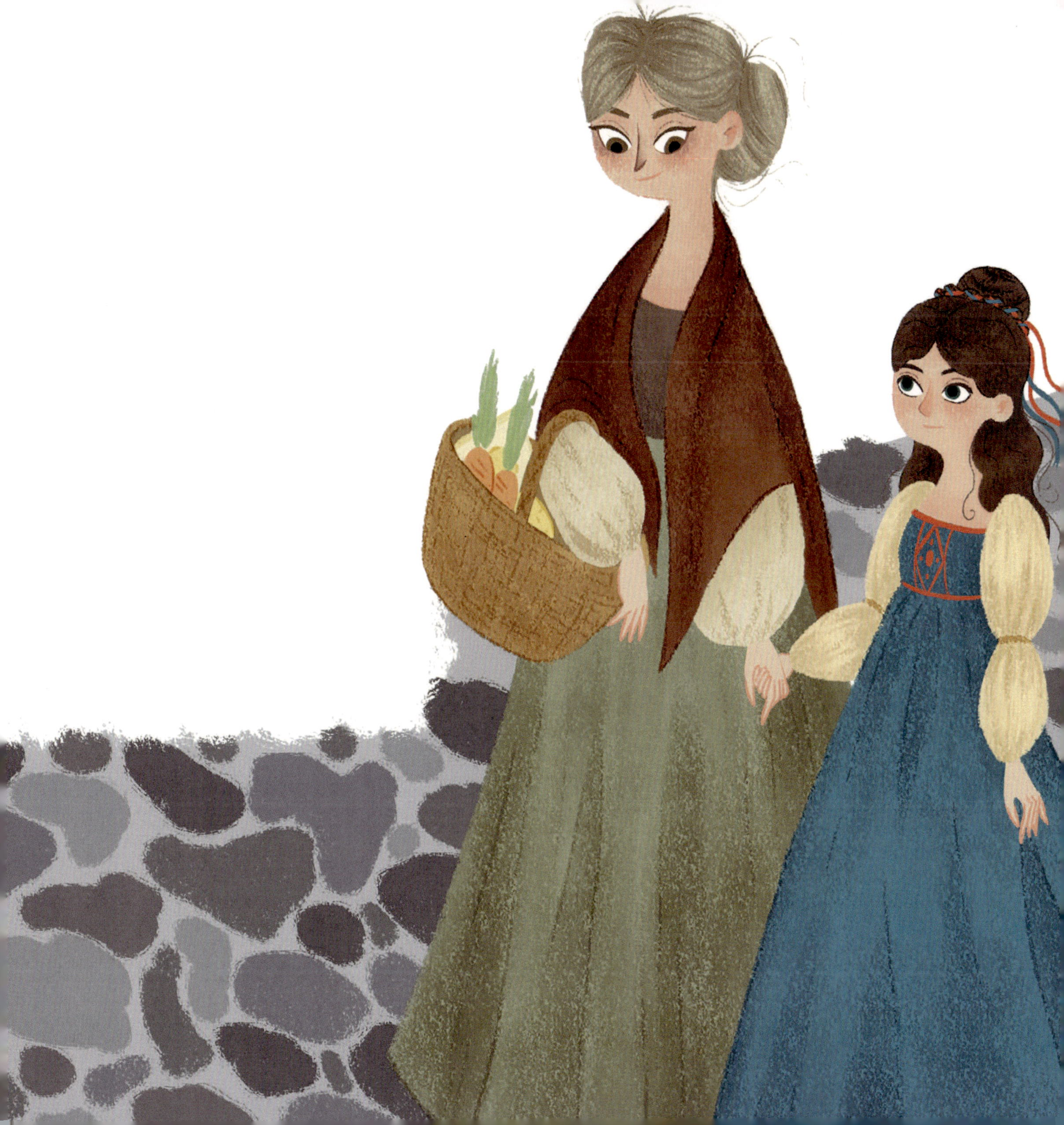

You knew your family lived a privileged life.

You saw many poor people working small plots of land on farms in the countryside, and you knew it was only a few generations ago that your family was struggling too. If they were lucky enough to be craftsmen or merchants, they belonged to a guild or union. The guild was created to protect both the workers and the patrons with a set of rules regulating prices. This made sure that no one was cheated and people had to use approved vendors.

Your grandfather created an expanding business that employed your father and all your uncles who lived next door with your cousins.

Grandfather bought silk from a merchant in Turkey, who had purchased it in China. You thought your grandpa was almost as rich as the Medici family because you lived in a big house with many servants.

The Medicis were his biggest customers. They had balls and parties and always needed new clothes. Your mama was excited when they invited her to do activities with the most important people of the town.

You lived in a house that was filled with beautiful things, including a few books made by a printer all the way in Germany! You used florino d'oro (flor-een-o de o-ro) or gold florins (flor-reens) to buy things in the Republic of Florence. Even though coins were minted everywhere in the world, the money from Florence was considered superior and accepted everywhere other currencies were not. In fact, one hundred and fifty European city-states made copies of it.

Clothes were a very important part of life in Florence. They were a display of your status in the town and an important symbol of your family's wealth.

As your parents owned a cloth shop, you were always outfitted in rich and embroidered fabrics. All of your siblings were dressed in the same clothes that adults wore, only in smaller sizes.

Your brothers were outfitted the same way as your father in colorful stockings called trousses (trou-sess). They were tightly fitted against their legs but ballooned out around their hips. Each wore a doublet (dub-let) which is a type of padded jacket made with rich fabrics like brocade and velvet. Everyone trimmed their clothes with ribbons and lace to make them stand out. A big cap with a feather completed the outfit, and men always wore a sporty cape called a mantle over one shoulder.

Your papa had a pointy beard but wore his hair closely cropped around his face. Your brothers looked like him, only without the beard!

31

You loved your long billowing dresses made with thick, bulky material. They could be made from the finest silk, damask, and brocades. It took a long time to get dressed with all the layers, starting with a petticoat (pet-ti-coat) which is a sort of slip you put on first. Over your petticoat, you put on a dress. It was high-waisted and close-fitted. You had big, puffy dramatic sleeves that ruffled down to your fingertips, making your arms look delicate. Your skirt was split in the front, showing your fancy embroidered, lace petticoat. There were pearls and precious gems sewn into the fabric making it very heavy to wear. Many of your garments were stitched with gold and silver thread so that you sparkled when the candlelight shone on your clothes.

You were luckier than the servant girls who only owned one change of clothes. Your mama employed a servant woman to keep your clothes clean and nice smelling. The woman tossed the clothes on bushes to dry in the hot sun. Your mama said it was important to keep diseases from coming into your home like they did in the olden days. The church also said to wash your hands in vinegar to prevent sickness from passing through the town. Florence was considered a clean city!

33

You had a pretty little cap decorated with gold chains, jewels, and feathers. It seemed a shame to cover the elegant hairstyle that your maid took hours to prepare. Your long, dark hair was rolled and braided so the heavy mass stayed in one place on your head. You wished your parents would let you bleach your hair blond like Mama's, but they said you weren't allowed until you were married. Mama's hair was so light, she looked like the angels the artists painted on the walls of the church. She carefully plucked out the hair on her hairline so that her forehead looked wide. All the stylish ladies painted their faces white with lead powder so they looked pale and elegant. Some people said the lead was not healthy, but beauty was more important than anything. Ground mother of pearl made a beautiful iridescent powder for Mama's eyelids. You loved to watch her dab her lips with vermillion (ver-mil-yun), a stain made from a red rock to make them bright red.

There was lots of fur and other adornments to stand out and show how important your family was. Your family was informed they could use fur, but to most others, it was forbidden. Only important people in town were allowed to display fur on their clothes.

35

Life was fun, and there was plenty to do, even if you weren't allowed to go out alone. There were sporting events, festivals, and dances. You learned how to play chess and checkers with your brothers. You loved singing or listening to music with your friends.

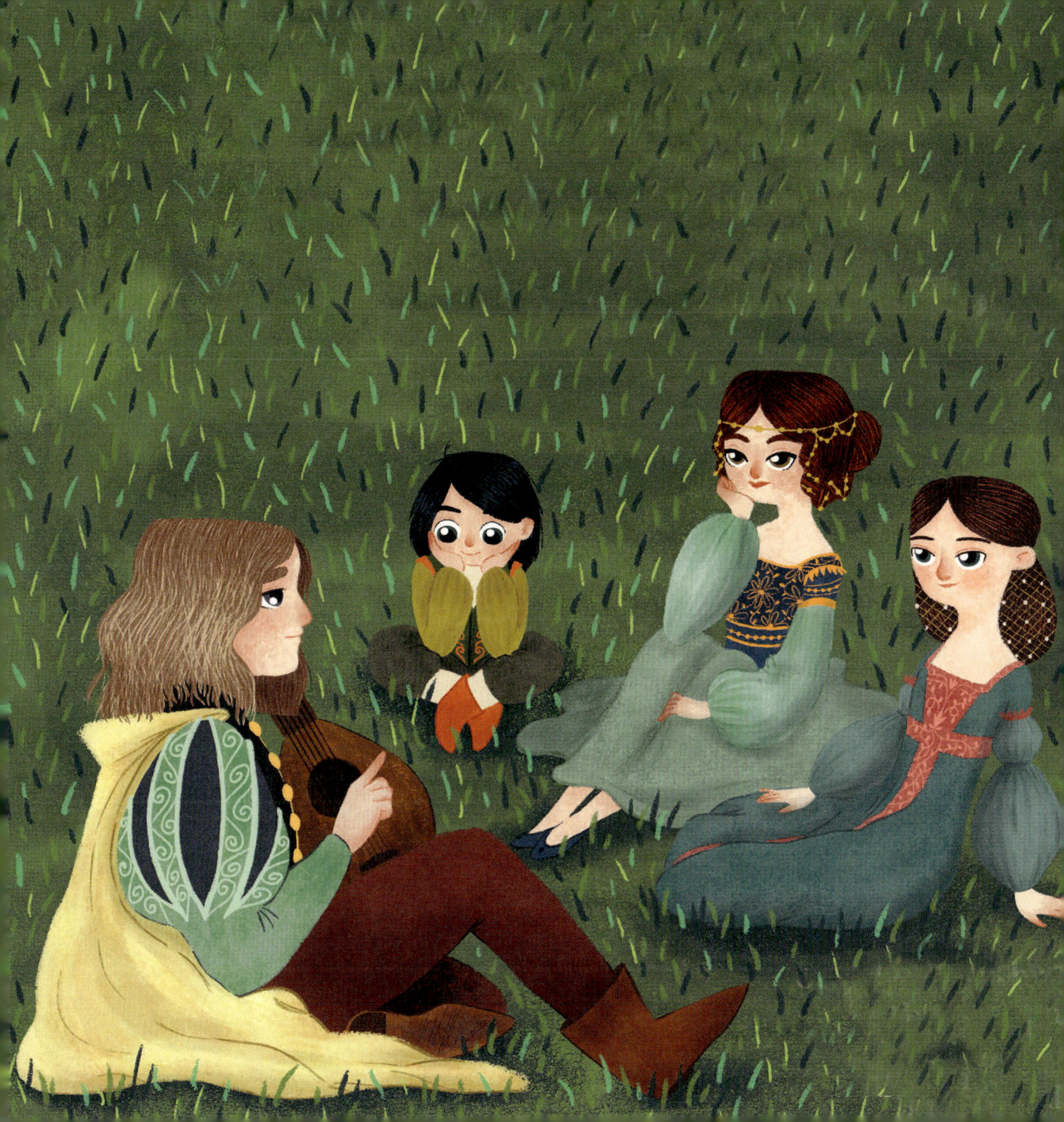

Every year before Lent, you loved the giant carnival that took place. There were parties where you dressed in costumes for a masquerade ball. You wore a mask, and your cousins had to guess who you pretended to be.

A new dance was devised, and you learned the steps so you shined the best when you performed the ballet with your partners. The strange stringed instrument called the violin, invented by Andrea Amati (An-drei-a A-ma-tee), made you feel as though you floated when you danced. You loved its rich and mournful sound.

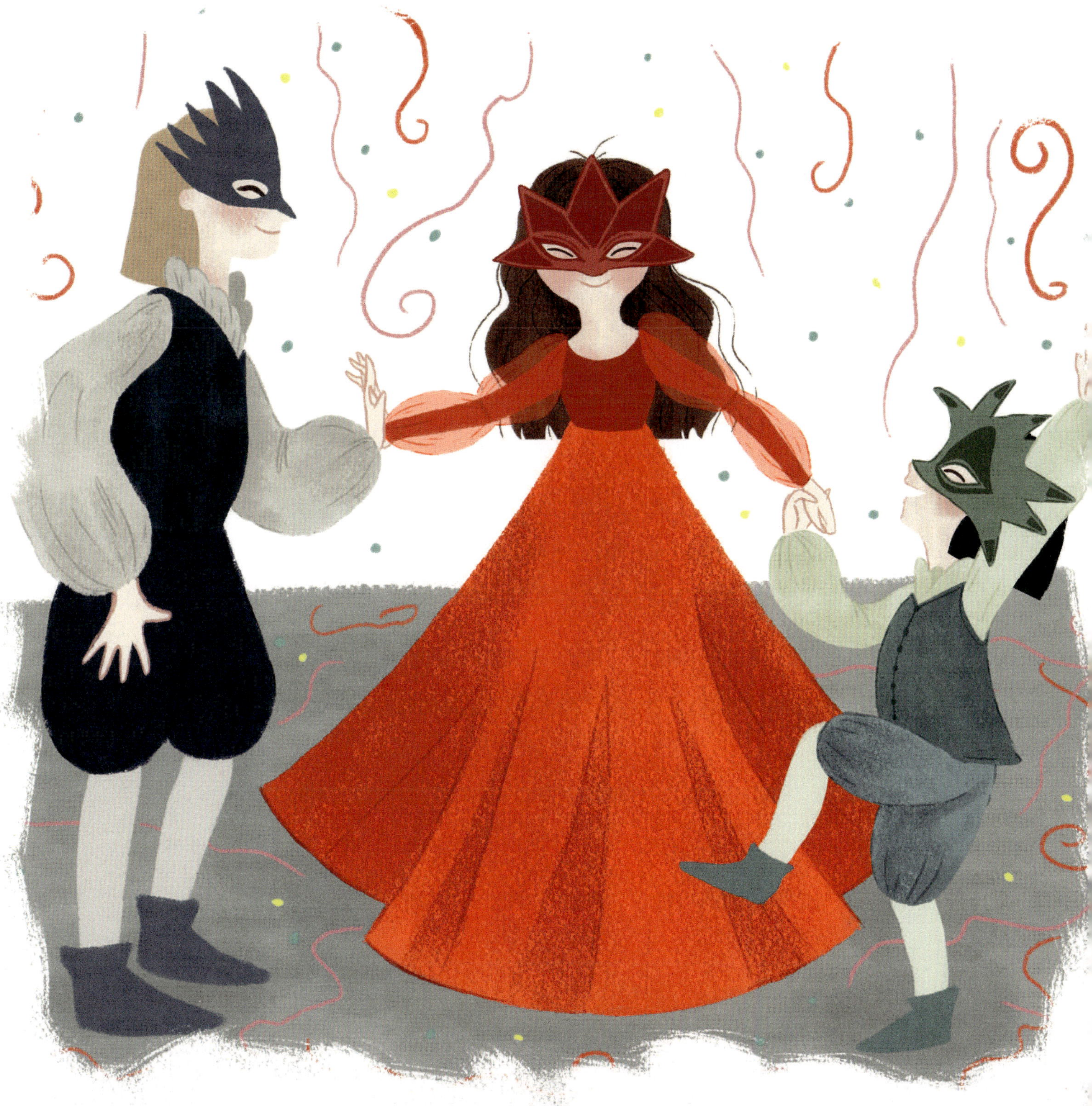

So you see, if you were me, how life in Renaissance Italy could really be.

Why was the Renaissance so important in art?

There were several artists and inventors who shaped the Renaissance era. You were proud to know about them because your papa always invited new ideas to be talked about at the supper table.

Art was changing during this time period, and it was thrilling to watch the new styles take shape. Many ideas were introduced to enhance the quality and realism of the art.

One of these styles was called perspective. This meant that the artist was drawing or painting a picture so that it looked like there were three dimensions. It gave the illusion that some objects in the painting were further away than others.

The other important change was balance and proportion. The artist drew subjects so that they were the correct size when compared

David by Donatello

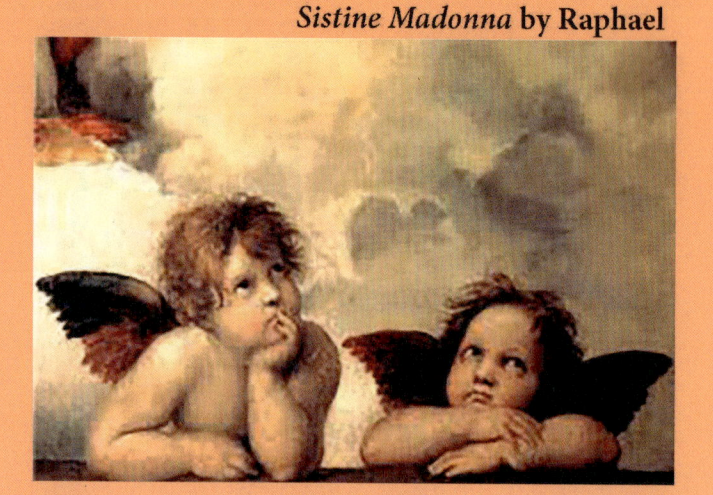

Sistine Madonna by Raphael

42

Hands of God & Adam by Michelangelo

David by Michelangelo

to each other.

Painters added the important use of light and dark called chiaroscuro (chi-a-ro-scu-ro).

Many artists started shading in their works to add drama and depth.

They learned by copying classical artists who created subjects to look life-like.

In the Middle Ages almost all European art was about religion, specifically Christianity and the Catholic Church. Renaissance artists painted many religious paintings. They also chose to include other subjects including Greek and Roman mythology, historical subjects, and portraits of individuals. They focused on the details of living, such as going to markets, dining, dancing, and creating pictures of everyday life.

One of the big changes in art was to

paint and sculpt subjects so they resembled actual people. This was called realism and involves a number of techniques that make marble look more like a person and their facial features seem more life-like.

Mona Lisa by Leonardo Da Vinci

Vitruvian Man by Leonardo Da Vinci

Famous People from the Italian Renaissance

The Renaissance changed the direction and thought process of the world. The great thinkers of the time influenced how we think today. The following is a group of those important people who shaped the world.

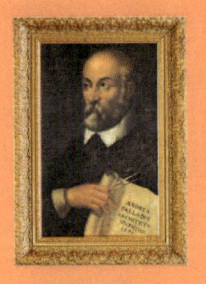

Andrea Palladio (An-drei-a Puh-lah-dee-o)- (1508-1580) was an Italian architect. Influenced by Roman and Greek architecture, Palladio was considered to be the most influential individual in the history of architecture. His clean lines and classical style greatly shaped the Renaissance movement throughout the world in architecture.

Artemisia Gentileschi (Art-te-miz-ja Gen-til-esh-kee)- (1593-1652) was one of the most famous female artist of the Renaissance. She was trained by her father when all the art academies refused to allow her to study because she was a woman.

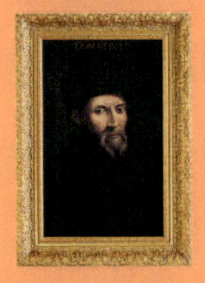

Donatello (Don-a-tel-lo)- (1386-1466) was actually *Donato di Niccolo di Betto Bardi*. He was an Italian painter and sculptor who was an important figure in the Renaissance. He created dramatic and emotional sculptures.

Filippo Brunelleschi (Fe-li-po Brun-el-she)- (1377-1446) was considered the first Renaissance architect. Some people say the Renaissance started when he was chosen to build the dome above the cathedral of Florence. This cone-shaped feature was the largest dome built since the Pantheon in Ancient Rome and still is the greatest feature in Florence's skyline. Brunelleschi also designed other churches in Florence. His designs were built with symmetry and order. Many more churches throughout Europe would copy his style in the following years.

Galileo Galilei (Ga-lee-lei-o Ga-lil-ee)- (1564-1642) was an astronomer, philosopher, and scientist who was called the "father of astronomy." He discovered four of the planet Jupiter's moons and was to first to observe and study sunspots. His ideas were considered contrary to popular beliefs of the Church, and they considered him a heretic. They put him on trial, and he was sentenced to house arrest for the rest of his life.

Isabella d'Este (Iz-a-bel-la d Es-tee)- (1474-1579) was the daughter of a wealthy nobleman and granddaughter of the King of Naples. She married a very important and powerful duke. She represented the what the Renaissance was all about. Highly educated, she became a famous hostess. She helped her husband by making important dinners inviting many people to discuss politics. She set important trends that developed art, music, and fashion of the time period.

Leonardo Da Vinci (Le-on-ar-do Da Vin-chee)- (1452-1519) was a painter, scientist, and inventor. Da Vinci is widely regarded as one of the greatest minds the world has ever produced. He was interested in everything from music to art and science. Da Vinci was a big influence on the Renaissance period. Amongst his many works was the painting, *The Mona Lisa*, and his sketch called *Vitruvian (Vi-tru-vian) Man*. He studied biology and how people moved to get his portraits as realistic as possible. Nowadays, they call someone a Renaissance Man when they are skilled at everything they do. Leonard was the definition of a Renaissance Man.

Lorenzo de' Medici (Lo-ren-zo de Me-dee-chee)- (1449-1492) was an Italian ruler of Florence. He was one of the most powerful supporters of the Renaissance. Also known as *Lorenzo the Magnificent,* he was a businessman, diplomat, and a patron of artists, poets, and scholars. He sponsored the newest and most daring artists, such as Botticelli (Bot-ti-chel-lee) and Michelangelo (Mik-ale-an-gel-o).

Michelangelo (Mike-ale-an-gel-o)- (1475-1564) was born as *Michelangelo di Lodovico Buonarroti Simoni* and was a Renaissance sculptor, painter, and architect. Michelangelo is often identified as the spirit of the Renaissance. His greatest works include the statue of David and his painting on the entire ceiling of the Sistine Chapel (Sis-teen Chap-uhl). It took four years to paint the ceiling chapel. Of the three hundred people in the painting, no two look alike. He also painted *The Last Judgment,* a famous painting on the wall of the Sistine Chapel. He was a poet who wrote hundreds of poems.

Niccolo Machiavelli (Nik-co-lo Mak-a-vel-lee)- (1469-1527) was an Italian writer, historian, diplomat, and humanist. He moved in political circles and created a new concept of political leaders based on a new perspective. His greatest work, *The Prince,* is about the world leaders of the time and the way they ruled their countries.

Raphael (Ra-fay-ale)- (1483-1520) was another Italian painter whose real name was *Raffaello Sanzio da Urbino*. He was one of three members of the Renaissance group of painters that defined the era. Raphael was asked by Pope Julius II to work on rooms in the Vatican at the same time as Michelangelo worked on the Sistine Chapel. Raphael was known for the perfection of his classical interpretations.

Sofonisba Anguissola (So-fon-es-ba An-gues-so-la)- (1532-1625) was educated with her sisters in fine art. She traveled to Rome and met with Michelangelo. She was invited to the Spanish court to paint, becoming the painting tutor to the queen.

Glossary

ale (aye-l)- a beverage similar to beer.

altar cloth (awl-ter kloth)- an embroidered cloth to cover and protect an altar in a church.

Andrea Amati- (An-drei-a A-ma-tee)- a man from Cremona, Italy, who was the first to invent an instrument similar to what we know today as the violin.

Andrea Palladio (An-drei-a Puh-lah-dee-o)- an Italian architect.

architect (ar-ki-tect)- a person who designs buildings.

architecture (ar-ki-tech-ture)- a general term to describe buildings or structures.

astronomy (uh-stron-uh-mee)- the study of the objects in the night sky and the universe.

balance (bal-uhn-ce)- an even distribution in art involving light, color, and placement.

ballet (ba-lay)- a type of graceful performance dance that began in the 15th century Renaissance courts and developed into the art form today.

betrothed (bih-trawtht)- engaged to be married.

Botticelli (Bot-ti-chel-lee)- an Italian painter.

brocade (bro-kaid)- a richly woven cloth.

carnival (car-nee-val)- a traditional Christian holiday and feast right before the start of Lent.

chiaroscuro (chi-a-ro-scu-ro)- the contrasting of light and shadow in artwork giving it character and depth.

china (chi-nuh)- a mix of bone, ash, and clay that makes delicate pottery.

cinnamon (sin-uh-min)- a spice made from the bark of special trees.

city-state (cit-tee-state)- a city that governs the surrounding territory.

cloves (klo-ves)- flower buds used as a spice.

Cosimo (Coh-zi-mo)- a popular boy's name in 15th century Florence.

damasks (dam-asks)- patterned fabrics made by weaving.

Dark Ages (Dah-ark Ages)- a time period referring to the Middle Ages when the Roman Empire declined and the society was said to have deteriorated.

Dolce (Dohl-chey)- a popular girl's name in 15th century Florence. It means sweet.

dome (dom)- usually on top of a building, a hollow half of a sphere or round shape.

doublet (dub-let)- a short, close-fitting padded jacket.

dowry (dow-ry)- money supplied by a bride's family to her husband upon marriage.

embroider (em-broi-der)- decorating cloth by sewing patterns on it with thread.

estate (eh-state)- land and property.

Firenze (Fi-ren-ze)- the Italian name for Florence. It is the capital of the Italian region of Tuscany.

Florence (Fi-ren-ze)- the capital of the Italian region of Tuscany. The birthplace of the Italian Renaissance.

florino d'oro (flor-een-o de o-ro)- the currency of 15th century Florence.

florins (flor-eens)- golden coins- currency.

fresco (fres-ko)- a painting of a mural on a wall covered with wet plaster.

gothic (goth-ik)- a Medieval art style that is heavy and ornate.

guild (gild)- a group of merchants or artists who control their craft in their hometown.

heretic (huh-ret-ik)- a person who had an opinion that went against popular thought.

humanism (hyoo-man-iz-um)- a concept that people are important in their own decision making rather than depending on religion.

Lent (Lent)- a Christian holiday that takes place six weeks before Easter where the focus is on simple living, prayer, and fasting.

Lisabetta (Liz-a-bet-ta)- a popular girl's name in 15th century Florence.

loggia (law-jah)- a covered corridor supported by a series of columns.

Lorenzo (Luh-renz-oh)- a popular boy's name in 15th century Florence.

mantle (man-tl)- a men's cloak that was worn over shoulder.

masquerade (mas-kuh-rade)- a costume ball (party) where men and women covered their faces with masks as a part of their costume.

Medici (Me-di-chee)- a famous family of bankers and rulers of Florence.

Medieval (Med-eve-val)- a period of time lasting from the 5th to the 15th centuries. It began with the collapse of the Roman Empire and ended with the beginning of the Renaissance.

merchant (mer-chent)- a person involved in bringing product to a market to sell or trade.

mother of pearl- the material from the inside of a sea shell. When ground into a powder it is beautiful, shiny and was used for cosmetics.

mythology (myth-ol-uh-gee)- stories that explain what people may not have been able to understand.

needlepoint (nee-dil point)- a stitched design on canvas used for decoration.

nutmeg (nut-meg)- the egg-shaped seed of the tree used as spice.

palazzo (pa-lah-tzo)- a very large and grand home.

Pantheon (Pan-thee-on)- a famous building in Rome completed in the year 126 A.D. It means "house of many gods."

perspective (per-spec-tive)- the art of drawing something so that it looks the correct size compared to other objects in the painting.

petticoat (pet-ti-coat)- a skirt-like undergarment that was made to be seen as part of a woman's outfit.

philosopher (phil-os-of-fer)- a person who studies the nature of life and human knowledge.

philosophy (phil-os-of-fee)- the study of the nature of life, existence, and knowledge.

porcelain (por-suh-lin)- a white translucent ceramic.

proportion (pro-por-shun)- sizing objects so they have the proper corresponding relationship.

realism (re-al-ism)- making something appear as true to life as possible, authentic.

Renaissance (Ren-ai-san-ce)- the European historical time period from the 14th through the 17th century which focuses on the new found interests of science, ancient art, and literature.

revolutionary (rev-o-lu-tion-ar-y)- a total change from an accepted way of life.

saffron (saf-run)- an orange-yellow spice made from the stigmas of the crocus flower.

sala (sah-la)- a salon or living room.

Sistine Chapel (Sis-teen Chap-uhl)- the Chapel in the official home of the Pope in Rome.

status (sta-tus)- high position or rank in society.

"The Athens of the Middle Ages" ("the Ath-inz of the Mid-l Ages) - Florence's nickname because it was the birthplace of the Italian Renaissance.

The Prince (The Prins)- a famous book written by Niccolo Machiavelli describing how a ruler should govern successfully.

trencher (tren-chur)- a flat round of bread used as a plate.

trousses (trou-sess)- colorful tights men wore as pants.

Tuscany (Tus-ca-nee)- the middle region of Italy and birthplace of the Italian

Renaissance.

vaulted (vawl-tid)- a large room built with high, arched roof, ceiling and walls.

velvet (vel-vit)- a short dense fabric that is soft to touch.

vermillion (ver-mil-yun)- red coloring made from a red rock called cinnabar.

vinegar (vin-ah-ger)- a liquid made from fermenting a fruit and used for cleaning hands in the Renaissance.

Vitruvian (Vi-tru-vian)- the famous sketch of a perfectly proportioned man made by Leonardo Da Vinci.

Please visit my blog for additional resources for this book and others, including printable worksheets, coloring pages, topics for essays and critical thinking.

caroleproman.blogspot.com

Made in the USA
Lexington, KY
27 January 2019